PLANT JOURNAL

THIS BELONGS TO:

_____

PLANT NAME

TYPE   **SCIENTIFIC NAME**

HISTORY OF THE PLANT

_____

_____

_____

_____

_____

SPECIAL CARE INSTRUCTIONS

_____

_____

_____

_____

_____

WATERING LOG

NOTES

LIGHTING LOG

NOTES

FERTILIZING AND REPOTTING LOG

NOTES

PLANT NAME

TYPE   **SCIENTIFIC NAME**

HISTORY OF THE PLANT

___

___

___

___

___

SPECIAL CARE INSTRUCTIONS

___

___

___

___

___

WATERING LOG

NOTES

LIGHTING LOG

NOTES

FERTILIZING AND REPOTTING LOG

NOTES

PLANT NAME

TYPE **SCIENTIFIC NAME**

HISTORY OF THE PLANT

_____
_____
_____
_____
_____

SPECIAL CARE INSTRUCTIONS

_____
_____
_____
_____
_____

WATERING LOG

NOTES

LIGHTING LOG

NOTES

FERTILIZING AND REPOTTING LOG

NOTES

PLANT NAME

TYPE **SCIENTIFIC NAME**

HISTORY OF THE PLANT

_____
_____
_____
_____
_____

SPECIAL CARE INSTRUCTIONS

_____
_____
_____
_____
_____

WATERING LOG

NOTES

LIGHTING LOG

NOTES

FERTILIZING AND REPOTTING LOG

NOTES

PLANT NAME

_____

TYPE　　　　　　**SCIENTIFIC NAME**

_____　　_____

HISTORY OF THE PLANT

_____

_____

_____

_____

_____

SPECIAL CARE INSTRUCTIONS

_____

_____

_____

_____

_____

_____

WATERING LOG

NOTES

LIGHTING LOG

NOTES

FERTILIZING AND REPOTTING LOG

NOTES

PLANT NAME

TYPE   **SCIENTIFIC NAME**

HISTORY OF THE PLANT

_____
_____
_____
_____
_____

SPECIAL CARE INSTRUCTIONS

_____
_____
_____
_____
_____

WATERING LOG

NOTES

LIGHTING LOG

NOTES

FERTILIZING AND REPOTTING LOG

NOTES

PLANT NAME

_____

TYPE **SCIENTIFIC NAME**

_____ _____

HISTORY OF THE PLANT

_____
_____
_____
_____
_____

SPECIAL CARE INSTRUCTIONS

_____
_____
_____
_____
_____
_____

WATERING LOG

NOTES

LIGHTING LOG

NOTES

FERTILIZING AND REPOTTING LOG

NOTES

PLANT NAME

TYPE **SCIENTIFIC NAME**

🌿 HISTORY OF THE PLANT 🌿

_____

_____

_____

_____

_____

🌿 SPECIAL CARE INSTRUCTIONS 🌿

_____

_____

_____

_____

_____

WATERING LOG

NOTES

LIGHTING LOG

NOTES

FERTILIZING AND REPOTTING LOG

NOTES

PLANT NAME

TYPE   **SCIENTIFIC NAME**

HISTORY OF THE PLANT

_____
_____
_____
_____
_____

SPECIAL CARE INSTRUCTIONS

_____
_____
_____
_____
_____
_____

WATERING LOG

NOTES

LIGHTING LOG

NOTES

FERTILIZING AND REPOTTING LOG

NOTES

PLANT NAME

TYPE **SCIENTIFIC NAME**

HISTORY OF THE PLANT

_____

_____

_____

_____

SPECIAL CARE INSTRUCTIONS

_____

_____

_____

_____

_____

WATERING LOG

NOTES

LIGHTING LOG

NOTES

FERTILIZING AND REPOTTING LOG

NOTES

PLANT NAME

TYPE **SCIENTIFIC NAME**

HISTORY OF THE PLANT

_____
_____
_____
_____
_____

SPECIAL CARE INSTRUCTIONS

_____
_____
_____
_____
_____

WATERING LOG

NOTES

LIGHTING LOG

NOTES

FERTILIZING AND REPOTTING LOG

NOTES

PLANT NAME

_____

TYPE   **SCIENTIFIC NAME**

_____   _____

HISTORY OF THE PLANT

_____
_____
_____
_____
_____

SPECIAL CARE INSTRUCTIONS

_____
_____
_____
_____
_____

WATERING LOG

NOTES

LIGHTING LOG

NOTES

FERTILIZING AND REPOTTING LOG

NOTES

PLANT NAME

TYPE   **SCIENTIFIC NAME**

HISTORY OF THE PLANT

_____

_____

_____

_____

_____

SPECIAL CARE INSTRUCTIONS

_____

_____

_____

_____

_____

_____

WATERING LOG

NOTES

LIGHTING LOG

NOTES

FERTILIZING AND REPOTTING LOG

NOTES

PLANT NAME

TYPE **SCIENTIFIC NAME**

HISTORY OF THE PLANT

_____
_____
_____
_____
_____

SPECIAL CARE INSTRUCTIONS

_____
_____
_____
_____
_____

WATERING LOG

NOTES

LIGHTING LOG

NOTES

FERTILIZING AND REPOTTING LOG

NOTES

PLANT NAME

TYPE   **SCIENTIFIC NAME**

HISTORY OF THE PLANT

_____
_____
_____
_____
_____

SPECIAL CARE INSTRUCTIONS

_____
_____
_____
_____
_____
_____

WATERING LOG

NOTES

LIGHTING LOG

NOTES

FERTILIZING AND REPOTTING LOG

NOTES

PLANT NAME

TYPE

SCIENTIFIC NAME

HISTORY OF THE PLANT

SPECIAL CARE INSTRUCTIONS

WATERING LOG

NOTES

LIGHTING LOG

NOTES

FERTILIZING AND REPOTTING LOG

NOTES

PLANT NAME

TYPE   **SCIENTIFIC NAME**

HISTORY OF THE PLANT

_____
_____
_____
_____
_____

SPECIAL CARE INSTRUCTIONS

_____
_____
_____
_____
_____

WATERING LOG

NOTES

LIGHTING LOG

NOTES

FERTILIZING AND REPOTTING LOG

NOTES

PLANT NAME

TYPE **SCIENTIFIC NAME**

HISTORY OF THE PLANT

_____

_____

_____

_____

_____

SPECIAL CARE INSTRUCTIONS

_____

_____

_____

_____

_____

WATERING LOG

NOTES

LIGHTING LOG

NOTES

FERTILIZING AND REPOTTING LOG

NOTES

PLANT NAME

TYPE   **SCIENTIFIC NAME**

HISTORY OF THE PLANT

SPECIAL CARE INSTRUCTIONS

WATERING LOG

NOTES

LIGHTING LOG

NOTES

FERTILIZING AND REPOTTING LOG

NOTES

PLANT NAME

TYPE **SCIENTIFIC NAME**

HISTORY OF THE PLANT

_____

_____

_____

_____

_____

SPECIAL CARE INSTRUCTIONS

_____

_____

_____

_____

_____

WATERING LOG

NOTES

LIGHTING LOG

NOTES

FERTILIZING AND REPOTTING LOG

NOTES

PLANT NAME

TYPE   **SCIENTIFIC NAME**

HISTORY OF THE PLANT

_____

_____

_____

_____

_____

SPECIAL CARE INSTRUCTIONS

_____

_____

_____

_____

_____

_____

WATERING LOG

NOTES

LIGHTING LOG

NOTES

FERTILIZING AND REPOTTING LOG

NOTES

PLANT NAME

TYPE   **SCIENTIFIC NAME**

HISTORY OF THE PLANT

_____
_____
_____
_____
_____

SPECIAL CARE INSTRUCTIONS

_____
_____
_____
_____
_____

WATERING LOG

NOTES

LIGHTING LOG

NOTES

FERTILIZING AND REPOTTING LOG

NOTES

PLANT NAME

TYPE SCIENTIFIC NAME

HISTORY OF THE PLANT

SPECIAL CARE INSTRUCTIONS

WATERING LOG

NOTES

LIGHTING LOG

NOTES

FERTILIZING AND REPOTTING LOG

NOTES

PLANT NAME

TYPE **SCIENTIFIC NAME**

HISTORY OF THE PLANT

_____
_____
_____
_____

SPECIAL CARE INSTRUCTIONS

_____
_____
_____
_____
_____

WATERING LOG

NOTES

LIGHTING LOG

NOTES

FERTILIZING AND REPOTTING LOG

NOTES

PLANT NAME

TYPE   **SCIENTIFIC NAME**

HISTORY OF THE PLANT

_____
_____
_____
_____

SPECIAL CARE INSTRUCTIONS

_____
_____
_____
_____
_____

WATERING LOG

NOTES

LIGHTING LOG

NOTES

FERTILIZING AND REPOTTING LO

NOTES

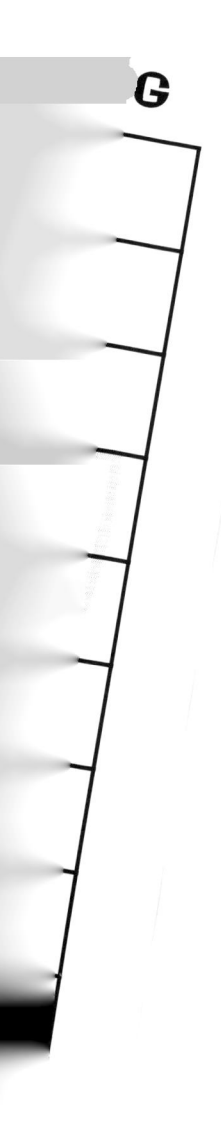

Printed in Great Britain
by Amazon